I Know I Can!
Tie My Laces

ANTHEA DAVIDSON-JARRETT
Illustrated by
Aldana Penayo
Published by EDUCATE THE GLOBE,
London, UK, 2023.

ISBN: 978-1-913804-08-4

Copyright © 2023 Educate The Globe Limited. All rights reserved. No part of this book is to be reprinted, copied or stored in retrieval systems of any type, except by written permission from the author. Part of this book may, however, be used only in reference to support related documents or subjects.

I know I can do it!

Please can I help?

I want to do it all by myself!

Please can I try?

Can you show me how?

I'm not too small,

I am ready right now!

I've bought a new pair

of the latest trainers.

Better than the ones worn

by the best entertainers!

But I'm not sure how

to tie my laces.

I tried very hard

and I've searched in all places!

My sister says that she

will show me how it's done.

She's going to put her trainers on

to teach me one on one.

Cross the laces over each other

because we're making a basic knot.

Now thread one lace in the space

under and pull tight, but not a lot!

Now again make the same basic knot.

This time we pull but then we stop

when you have made a circle just like this,

it's time for the bunny ears! We've got this!

Through the middle of the circle

thread one lace

then thread the second lace through

the same circle space.

Pull the end of each lace until you see

two bunny ears like leaves on a tree.

The easy part is next; we're nearly there.

This will take a few tries but never fear!

All that's left to do

is to pull the bunny ears tight!

I'll never trip on my laces

if I do this right!

There's another way too, if you want to try!

Like the first way, a basic knot you must tie.

Then you make two bunny ears with each lace.

Cross the ears over and under them you'll find a space.

Thread one of the ears through

the space under the cross

then pull both ears tight and

voila! You are the boss!

There are a few ways to tie

the laces of footwear.

Choose the one you like

and then practice with great care.

Soon enough you'll ace it

then you'll tie them with much flair!

You can teach your friends too if

they find it a nightmare!

But before we get there

you'll have to practise every day

so you can do it on your own

and be the master of your game.

When you know how

shout out loud "I SLAY!"

Smile at yourself in the mirror

and have the most brilliant day!

www.ingramcontent.com/pod-product-compliance
Lightning Source LLC
Chambersburg PA
CBHW041245240426
43670CB00027B/2995